S.O.S.

Children are a gift from God.
Enjoy!
Claire W. Miller

# Splashes of Serenity

### Bathtime Reflections for Drained Moms

Written by Elaine W. Miller

Photography by Sonny Sensor

**SPLASHES OF SERENITY**
BATHTIME REFLECTIONS FOR DRAINED MOMS

Written by Elaine W. Miller
Photography by Sonny Sensor

Published by Green Key Books

International Standard Book Number: 1-932587-56-X

Front Cover Photography: Stockbyte
Back Cover Photography: Brand X Pictures

Layout: David Gillaspie/Impact Productions
Project Management: JJ Graphics

Unless otherwise noted, all Scripture quotations are taken from GOD'S WORD® Translation, ©1995 God's Word to the Nations. Used by permission.

Scripture quotations marked (NIV) are taken from the HOLY BIBLE, NEW INTERNATIONAL VERSION® (NIV®). ©1973, 1978, 1984 by International Bible Society. Used by permission of Zondervan. All rights reserved.

For information:
GREEN KEY BOOKS
2514 ALOHA PLACE
HOLIDAY, FLORIDA 34691

Library of Congress Cataloging-in-Publication Data available upon request.

Printed in Italy

# Table of Contents

# No Room in the Tub for Me

*"Children are an inheritance from the Lord. They are a reward from him."*
—Psalm 127:3

Sleep deprived and weary, I push the floating toys aside, attempting to enjoy the luxury of a bubble bath. Toy boats, a rubber duck, bathtub paints, various sizes of plastic pitchers (mostly used to dump water on the floor), and a metal matchbox car (mostly used to scratch the bathtub surface) invade my territory. "Take Me Away" promises the bubble bath box. Eye to eye with the headlights of a matchbox car, I yearn to be taken away for just a short moment from the exhaustion of motherhood. The toys I float with deny me the pleasure of forgetting my forgettable day.

I remember the new coffee table with fresh teeth marks from the baby and milk spilling twice on my freshly mopped floor. Putting three little ones in snowsuits was enough aerobic activity to exhaust even the most buff body. Buff body? Well, that's one advantage of the bathtub toys. They hide this not-at-all buff body. I am tired and teary and wonder if the days of bathing with toys will ever end...

The toys are gone. The milk isn't spilled so much anymore, and snowsuits have all gone to the Salvation Army. I close my eyes and immerse into the toyless, hot, bubbly bathwater. Hoping to be "taken away," I relax. Peace is interrupted by floating bottles bobbing against my head. One eye opens to the truth that there is still no room in the tub for me. A myriad of shampoos, conditioners, oil treatments, and acne removers have replaced the bathtub toys. Concerns of dents in the car replace thoughts of teeth marks in the coffee table. I live in the world of teenagers, and the issues they face press hard on my heart. I close my ears to the radio blaring indistinguishable words from the small bedroom down the hall. Will the day ever come when I have the tub and my mind to myself?

The day has come sooner than I ever anticipated. Tomorrow my youngest leaves for college. I soak, peacefully, in the tub reflecting on the day. His hand held mine during the mealtime prayer. I confess this mother's heart was not thinking about the meal or the prayer. I was remembering my baby boy and wondering when his hands, so gently enclosing mine, grew to be so big. I remember his hands, smaller than mine, and the precious prayers of a little boy now grown to be a man. How quickly time passes and how precious each moment I have to cherish my child, God's reward to me.

Don't wish any days away, for "Wherever you are, be all there." These wise words of Jim Elliott, a missionary martyred before his only daughter's first birthday, speak to me.[1] We mothers need to enjoy each age and cherish every moment. Wherever we are on our motherhood journey, we need to "be all there."

Believe me, the spilled milk stops spilling, and our children do learn to put their snowsuits on themselves. The dents in the car are hammered out, and teeth marks in the coffee table become treasured memories and conversation pieces when spouses-to-be start arriving. All of those bathtub toys are replaced by a barrage of teenage hair products, and suddenly, the bathtub is empty. Finally, there is room in the tub for me. My eyes tear as I peacefully soak and miss the clutter.

*Dear Lord, help me seize the day. How little time I have to teach, train, and treasure your gift to me. One day I'll smile at the teeth marks and wish for finger and nose prints on my window. Help me to remember to "be all there" on my motherhood journey. Keep me from longing for the future and missing the joys of the present. You have given me a beautiful gift. Thank you. May I embrace each moment. In Jesus' name, amen.*

# Help! I'm Torn in Two Today

*"Husbands, love your wives, as Christ loved the church and gave his life for it. He did this to make the church holy by cleansing it, washing it using water along with spoken words. Then he could present it to himself as a glorious church, without any kind of stain or wrinkle—holy and without faults."*

—Ephesians 5:25-27, 33b

My arms ache from holding too much of my child and not enough of my husband. My mind is weary. My heart is tearing in two trying to balance my life—half mother and half wife. My husband loves me, but I sure don't feel "radiant...without stain or wrinkle or any other blemish" (NIV). My sweatsuit reeks of spoiled milk and spit-up cereal. My face is happy just to get washed and has lost all hope of ever seeing a facial mask. The clogged pores will just have to stay clogged. I determine it is impossible to satisfy the needs of both an infant in need of feeding and a husband in need of loving.

I'll mother instead of wife. The best is not to be torn in two. After all, my husband won't starve, and his personality has already been determined by his mother's love. My child's temperament, however, depends on me, and the baby can't walk to the fridge and fix her own bologna sandwich. I rationalize I am doing a pretty good job because I haven't even put my own needs into this equation.

When was the last time I did something just for me? I am quite the martyr. I am doing my best. But, am I doing God's best?

Sweetly, my husband comes to me. "We need to talk," he says. I realize he is not being selfish; he is being sensible when he pleads for some attention. He speaks of the love we both have for our child and the reality that a baby takes time and patience and is an adjustment to a marriage. "But what good will it do our baby, if we end up divorced?" he asks. Shocked to hear the word *divorced* from his lips, I realize it is spoken with love and concern for us as a couple. He is right.

The best thing we can do for our child is work at and preserve our marriage. My daughter will watch me and learn how to be a wife. I must respect my husband and make our relationship a priority. Nurturing a good marriage goes a long way toward nurturing a child. That is God's best.

*Lord, it is difficult to do all I have to do today. So many seem to be demanding my attention. Help me to keep my priorities right. May I love and respect my husband and not exasperate my children. Bind us together as a family. Help us to be sensitive to each other's needs. Give me time for myself, too. Most of all, give me a heart that both my husband and my children will find easy to love—one that radiates You.*

# Do You Know Where Your Children Are?

*"The Lord is fighting for you! So be still!"*
—Exodus 14:14

I don't know where my son is sleeping tonight. The silence coming from Sam's bedroom is so loud I cannot sleep. I toss and turn and pray. Sam went alone to Montana to experience his dream fly-fishing vacation. He left in our van with our blessing. How did we ever let that happen? He expects to be gone two weeks. Two weeks is a long time for a mother to go without sleep.

I remember another sleepless night when my husband was late in a snowstorm. Certain he was dead in a ditch, I planned his funeral, sold the house, and contemplated a career outside the home. So sure of my widowhood, it's amazing I didn't include a new husband in my arrangements.

Quiet houses and empty beds can be unsettling for a wife and mother who tends to worry. I would certainly like to have back all the time and effort I spent laying out funerals for very-much-alive loved ones.

"Worry does not empty tomorrow of its sorrow; it empties today of its strength," says Corrie ten Boom.[2] How true. If my son is in trouble in Montana, there is nothing I can do about it tonight in New York. I am weary of worry. I pray and remember God's Word that He will fight for my son. I need only be still. Peace then arrives, and sleep comes as I give my child back to the Heavenly Father.

How often we take on life's fights when the Lord says He will fight for us! We need only be still. As I sleep tonight, I enjoy stillness and good rest knowing the God who never sleeps is fighting my battles for me. And He never loses.

*Dear Lord, when I don't know where my children sleep, when someone I love is late in a storm, when things going on in my life cause me to worry and rob me of strength, I thank You that You are fighting for me. May I be still in Your arms tonight as You go off to battle, and I go off to sleep. Thank you, Lord.*

# God Never Says "Oops!"

*"You alone created my inner being. You knitted me together inside my mother."*
—Psalm 139:13

What was God doing the day He knit Garrett's lip in his mother's womb? Was He so busy solving other problems that he missed a few stitches? How easy for God to correct such a simple mistake. Perhaps God was so preoccupied putting extra stitches in Garrett's beautiful heart that He forgot about his lip.

My grandson was born with a cleft lip and palate. Everyone was surprised. The ultrasound did not show it; the doctors and nurses even missed it at Garrett's delivery. His mother was the first to notice as she attempted to nurse her son. Her hungry boy could not suck. As she gazed at her precious child, she was assured that God knit him perfectly in her womb. God did not say, "Oops! I missed a stitch."

Nor was God surprised when Gabrielle was born with five broken bones. Brittle bone disease was the diagnosis. Confidently, her mother proclaimed, "Gabrielle is God's good and perfect gift. God was in control on day one. I know God is in control of this." God didn't say "Oops!" when Gabrielle was born.

"Oops" isn't in God's vocabulary. He knows who, what, where, when, and how. He also knows why. He knows that imperfect lips and brittle bones can lead us into His arms, and sometimes, we need a good hug.

There were lots of hugs the day of the car accident. Careening into a creek, the car was totaled. Garrett's family was shaken but unhurt. Big brother, Connor, had to be taken to the emergency room just to make sure he was all right. What a thrill for a two year old! His dream of riding in an ambulance (which he thought was a school bus) came true. When we arrived at the emergency room, my husband and I were relieved to see our daughter and her family intact. Connor excitedly jumped into his grandpa's arms, gave him a big hug, and said, "It was fun, Grandpa!" Holding my daughter tightly, I whispered thanks to God that she was all right. She whispered back, "God didn't say 'Oops.' He knew all about it."

When we go through the accidents of life, we need to jump into our Heavenly Father's arms. And we hope when it is all over, we look back and say, "It was fun, God!" We will go for some rides in this life. We might as well go through them hugging Jesus. He isn't too busy, He isn't surprised, and He's still in control.

*Forgive me, Lord, for all of the times I may think You are saying, "Oops!" Cleanse my heart of doubt that You are in power. You created me, and You created this day. You know how it will begin and how it will end. There are no accidents in Your perfect plan. Thank You that You are knitting everything together according to Your will and for my good. Hold me and carry me through my days.*

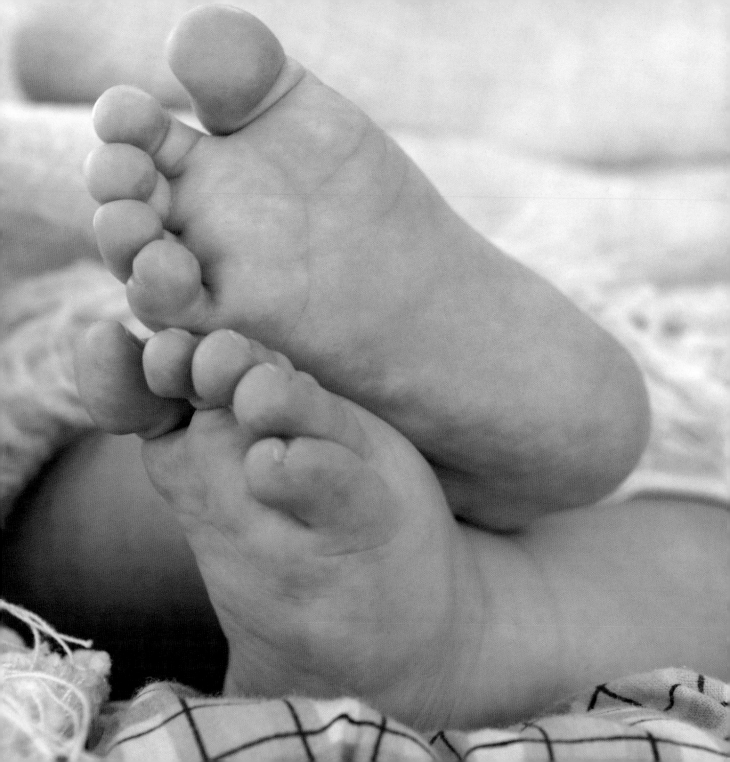

# My Feet are Tied

*"We can't allow ourselves to get tired of living the right way. Certainly, each of us will receive everlasting life at the proper time, if we don't give up."*

—Galatians 6:9

The four children in my charge have big plans for my baby sitting debut. Three hold me while one encircles my feet and the rest of my body with rope. Sufficiently bound, I am pushed into a dark closet. The door closes. A failure as a babysitter, I dread the return of trusting parents. Awaking from this teenage nightmare, I am thankful it is only a dream.

For too many mothers, this teenage apparition is middle-age reality. We feel like our children have tied us up, and we are living in a dark closet. Worse than that, we wish our children would tie us up and leave us alone in a dark closet. Worse yet, we desire to tie our children up and keep them in the closet. Every mother on one day or another feels weary. Mothering is tiresome. (That's why I hope you are reading this in a hot bubble bath. You deserve it, you know.)

In India, there is a saying that "children tie a mother's feet." Amy Carmichael spent her life modeling Jesus' sacrificial love. Children tied her feet over many years as she served in an orphanage in India. Amy wrote, "Babies tie a Mother's feet, so let our feet be tied for love of Him whose feet were pierced."[3] On days when Amy felt her feet were tied, she did not grow weary, she did not give up, she looked to Jesus whose feet were pierced, and she reaped a harvest.

It is difficult to run the race called life with our feet tied. We fall, awkwardly pick ourselves up, and soon fall again. Is it worth it? God thinks so. He cheers us on with words like "Don't grow weary...don't give up...you'll reap a harvest" (NIV). On days when we feel like our feet are tied and our stomach is in knots, remember Jesus. He didn't grow weary and give up. He is our perfect example of sacrificial love.

Imagine it. Jesus must have been weary anticipating the nails that would tie his feet to the cross, yet He kept on doing good. He washed His disciples' feet, knowing His feet would soon be washed with His own blood. If Jesus could do this for us, can't we take joy in washing a baby's ten toes for the umpteenth time? When days are too hard and we just want to lock ourselves in the closet, remember Jesus and what He did for us.

Jesus loves us so much that He died for us. He loves mothers so much that He entrusts them with His treasures—our babies. On weary days, look to Him. Ask Him for strength. He desires to come into our dark closet, loosen the ties around our feet, and give us a good foot washing. He'll massage our tired toes with oils of gladness and transform our sluggish steps into a joyful dance. He desires to run the race with us. We can't do it in our own strength, but with Jesus' help, we will win the race and reap a wonderful harvest even with our feet tied.

*Lord, I gladly have my feet tied for this time in my life. When the bindings get too tight, help me remember that You loved me so much that You allowed Your feet to be pierced. May I be willing to sacrifice for my children and love them as You sacrificed and loved me. Thank you, Jesus.*

# Sweet Surprises

*"A joyful heart is good medicine."*
—Proverbs 17:22a

Dessert was a rarity growing up at my house. My mother was very health conscious for a woman in the 1950's. Sugar was a "no-no." That's why I ran so fast and fell so quickly for any practical joke involving sweet food. Desserts came only on special occasions, but laughter was a daily occurrence.

As the fourth of six children, I fought hard to be first. I should have suspected something was amiss when my older siblings all too gladly allowed me the first bite of mom's candy. The chocolate was good with an added crunch to it. It didn't have the consistency of nuts or rice crispy cereal or coconut. Innocently, I asked about the crunch. "Ants!" my siblings and mother burst out the surprise. Not wanting them to have the upper hand, I confidently swallowed and said, "They're good. You should try some." Everyone, including me, burst out laughing. I silently shuddered and refused to mention the little buggers were sticking to my teeth.

Peanut brittle was my favorite treat. My mouth watered when I spied the can labeled "peanut brittle" hidden on the top shelf. *No one will notice if I have one small bite,* I assured myself as I climbed the chair in pursuit of peanuts and brittle. Standing on tippy toes on the kitchen counter, I could barely reach it. Amazed no one was around to see my act of thievery, I hoped the jar had been opened so that I could sneak a snack undetected. Aha! The seal was broken. There had been another culprit before me who secretly enjoyed the sugary treat. Carefully and quietly opening the lid, I screamed in surprise! Out of the can shot a three-foot coiled play snake. Two more followed, flying through the kitchen air landing wherever. I was caught. My spying siblings appeared from the next room in uproarious laughter.

What is the spiritual application here? Chocolate-covered ants and peanut brittle snakes can do more to promote good health than vegetables and vitamins. If laughter is good medicine, we need to plan moments of laughter with our families to keep them healthy. The world is filled with stress. Our homes need to be stress-free living zones and safe havens of laughter.

*Lord, I pray for my family. Fill our hearts with love and laughter. Make our home a place of emotional health. Help me to lighten up and laugh easily. Thank you, Lord, for the gift of laughter and the stress it relieves. May we daily take large doses of Your cheerful heart medicine. In Jesus' name, I pray with a smile on my face, laughter in my heart, and chocolate-covered ants possibly still lodging in my teeth.*

# Serving Tea in the Bathroom

*"[Love] isn't rude. It doesn't think about itself. It isn't irritable. It doesn't keep track of wrongs."*
—1 Corinthians 13:5

How quickly and foolishly I become angry. Tiny, muddy sneakers run on the freshly cleaned rug. My son is excited to share his new-found frog with his most-loved friend, Mommy. Yesterday, before the rug cleaning, I would have been thrilled with the frog. Today, I shriek thoughtless words of reprimand, "Don't come in here with those muddy shoes on my clean rug and don't bring that awful frog in the house!" My child's self worth sinks at the megaphoned message. In his mind he hears, "The rug is more important to me than you or your new friend, the frog."

How much of my anger has everything to do with what day the rug was cleaned and little to do with the wee one, only acting his age, desiring to share his prized possession with the most important person in his life? Even so, I have desires, too. I desire a clean rug. I desire not to have frogs in the house. Most of all, I desire for my children to know how deeply I love them.

Some of my other desires are too extravagant for a mother of three preschoolers. An afternoon to myself finds me in the China section of a department store. With no thought of actually purchasing anything, I walk among displays of expensive glass. There are no children here. This is an adult department. I enjoy the quiet. My eye catches sight of a China toothbrush holder that almost perfectly matches my bathroom wallpaper. How lovely it would look in my home. Forgetting that a rubber ducky is more appropriate for this stage of my life, I rationalize, *It will 'pick me up' while I pick up toys. It will 'boost my spirits' while I wash booster seats,* so I impulsively buy it.

I daily clean the toothpaste art from the hand-painted china. I won't let my mind think it isn't as pretty as in the store. Five slimy toothbrushes protruding out of five toothpaste-caked holes of a beautifully flowered toothbrush holder is really more comical than pleasurable. Growing tired of the endless washing ritual, I sigh, "I don't serve tea in the bathroom. Why would I have my china displayed there?"

Then, the inevitable happens. An innocent, sweet, five-year-old son tries to please Mommy and brush his teeth without help or reminder. The prize of all toothbrush holders crashes to the tile floor shattering more than the china piece. My son crouches in guilt and fear as I lash out at him in frustrated anger, "Can't I ever have anything nice?" The sadness on my little boy's face still plays on my mind years later. Do I care about the toothbrush holder? It is meaningless. Do I care about my son? He means the world to me. For a brief moment a toothbrush holder was more important. How stupid is that?

*Lord, cleanse my heart of anger and fill it with love. Be Lord of my heart and Lord of my tongue and keep me from saying words that hurt my little ones. I do need to discipline my children, but I don't need to destroy them. When things happen that won't even matter five days from now, help me keep a reign on my tongue. May material possessions never be more important than Your heavenly treasures. I need You to guide me each day and remind me that my children are irreplaceable and fragile. May they always feel loved. Jesus, thank You for Your love. Thank You that You don't become easily angered with me even when I break the hearts of your precious gifts. I love them, Jesus. Thank You for allowing me to be their mom.*

# Two Mothers—One Heart

*"Don't love money. Be happy with what you have because God has said, 'I will never abandon you or leave you."*

—Hebrews 13:5

Dreamily, she lies in her bathtub closing her eyes to the truth of her life situation. There's no money to repaper or paint the bathroom. The bathtub is stained and will remain that way. Her eyes close to the reality of the stark bathroom, but her mind won't close to the reality of her humble income. She can't afford to give her daughter any of the finer things. Will her lack of means harm her child? Will her daughter succeed? She feels a little more money will give her daughter a better life. Soaking in the tub, she yearns for a little more.

Across town, another mother soaks in a sunken whirlpool hot tub. Her eyes remain open enjoying the view of gardens from the windows surrounding her sanctuary. She lies back and gazes at heaven through the skylights above. Drinking in the serenity, her body is soothed, but her mind is unsettled. She wonders how her wealth will harm her child. How will her daughter succeed when everything is handed to her? She feels a little less money will be better for her daughter. Soaking in the tub, she yearns for a little less.

Two mothers, two lifestyles, share the same heart. They teach their daughters not to make material things their goal. "God is with you always, whether you are rich or poor, and He has a plan for your life. Contentment comes from being in God's will, not your income. Don't let money determine your life decisions." They teach these truths in word and deed, and both daughters learn their lessons well.

Years later, the wealthy girl has accumulated more wealth. She is smart, strong, sensible, and sensitive. Her heart is not greedy. Her heart is tender. She uses her riches to enrich others. Content and happy, she lies in her own sunken whirlpool hot tub looking through the skylights to heaven. She asks God how she should spend His money. He directs her to a missionary serving in a far-off country.

The young missionary is so thankful for the generous check. Smart, strong, sensible, and sensitive, she lies in her stained bathtub and closes her eyes to the walls in need of paint. She never knew or wanted anything better. Her heart is full of contentment. Shutting her eyes, she thanks God for her rich life and asks Him how to spend His money. He directs her to send a little home to her mother. After all, her bathroom needs painting.

*Lord, thank you for never charging admission to come into your presence. Thank You for looking at my heart, not my income. Whether I live richer or poorer, I know you are with me. I know Your plan includes contentment. You don't care what my paycheck reads, but You do care about my heart. Cleanse it, please. May I spend less time raising money and more time raising my children.*

*Lord, You have a plan for my children's lives. Whether they experience wealth or poverty, may the little ones be free from the love of money and content with what they have, knowing You will never leave them nor forsake them, for this is true wealth.*

# Smiling at Evil

*"[Love] isn't happy when injustice is done, but it is happy with the truth."*
—1 Corinthians 13:6

"Ooooo, Yuck! I don't want to touch that!" a young father declares as he whiffs his precious son's soiled diaper. Holding the baby with one hand and grasping the remote with the other, he proclaims, "Wow, look at that!" His eyes catch sight of a violent scene on the television, and he can't seem to break away from its evil enticement...

"I'm not eating green trees!" A teenager protests the broccoli on his plate. Wondering if he could qualify as a contestant, he hurries through dinner hoping to watch people eating worms on the latest reality show...

"I won't get a bath in that dirty water!" My six-year-old voice sobbed. None of my five siblings nor I wanted to be last in the bathtub. A dry summer had our well dangerously low, so we shared bathwater that August. The day the rain finally arrived we ran outside to cover ourselves with fresh showers and slop in new mud. Bathing with dirty worms seemed delightful...

We humans are strange—saying one thing yet doing another. As we seek to teach our children moral values, we hope they will agree that evil has no place in our homes, hearts, or minds. All the while, they are watching to see what makes us happy. Our children learn from us what gives us pleasure.

So what do our children see us delight in? What makes us smile? Are we more excited about the dream vacation than the worship service? Do we tell our little ones to hush their enthusiastic questions so we won't miss the marriage proposal on our favorite sitcom? Have we rushed our children to bed, hurried through a story, and mumbled a thoughtless night-night prayer so we can return to our romance novel? Are we excited when we have a hot piece of gossip to convey over the telephone?

God says, "Love does not delight in evil, but rejoices with the truth" (1 Corinthians 13:6 NIV). Although none of the above is necessarily "evil," it is good to evaluate the word *truth* as the standard by which we measure our activities. What is it we are to rejoice in? Jesus said, "I am the way, the truth, and the life" (John 14:6), and we know that His written Word is truth (John 17:17). In the Bible, Jesus speaks truth to us about God, marriage, children, and trials in life.

So do our children see us rejoice in these things? Does praying and reading God's Word put a smile on our face? Do our children see in our eyes how much we treasure them as heavenly gifts created by God? Do they see us beam at the sight of our beloved husband? Do they observe the respect that we have for our husbands? Do they see us rejoice when a trial tests our trust in a God who loves us and promises to work all things out for our good? They need to see that joy comes from our relationship with a loving God. They need to realize from our lives that happiness comes from knowing Jesus as Lord and Savior.

The world is filled with evil enticements. May we find no entertainment in them. Let us examine ourselves often to see what makes us smile.

*Dear Lord, I don't want to wallow in the mud. I don't want shallow stuff to intrude upon my day and rob me of the deep pleasures You have planned for me. Cleanse me of my evil desires. Fill my eyes and heart and mind with rejoicing in the true things—the eternal things—that You give me. Help me to make right choices. May my children know they are treasured and never see me take pleasure in evil.*

# God's Tattoo

*"Will she have no compassion on the child from her womb? Although mothers may forget, I will not forget you. I have engraved you on the palms of my hands."*

—Isaiah 49:15b–16a

Standing in the shower, she can't miss the red rose tattooed on her right thigh. Four children and fifteen years later, she wishes the rose would disappear. The flower is beginning to wrinkle along with her skin. We all do silly things when we are young—when life is carefree and our only concern seems to be which hip would best boast the rose.

Today, her heart is heavy with more pressing matters. "Oh, God, why is my baby so sick? Why is this happening to me? Let me suffer, not my sweet, sweet baby," she pleads a prayer as she weeps in the water. Agonizing, in physical and emotional exhaustion, she screams at God, "God, I love You. I trust You. I know all the verses. I know everything will work out for my good. I want to obey You and be thankful through this most awful trial of my life. But, God, I am not fine! My heart is breaking!"

In the midst of her sobful prayer, she senses His presence. In her heart, she hears His gentle voice say, "My dear child, you are not fine. But you are still mine. Your heart may break, but your spirit will not." With her head hanging low under the weight of her pain, her eyes notice the red rose tattoo. God reminds her that He, too, has a tattoo. He has engraved her and her baby in the palm of His hand. He has promised, "I will not forget you! I will not forget your baby!" As her eyes look up to Jesus, His Spirit consumes her with peace as the shower washes away her tears. For the first time in years, she is glad for the rose tattoo. It will never wash away, nor will God's tattoo of her.

*Wow, God has a tattoo of me! Much better, He has a tattoo of my baby! He has promised never to forget me. Thank You, Lord, that when life seems too hard to bear You are there. When I am not fine, I am still Yours. Thank You that You are with my children. You created them and know everything about them. You know where they are right now, and You have promised You will not forget them. Thanks for engraving them on the palms of Your hands—just in case You need a reminder and I know You don't. You are God. You are my God. I trust You and love You even on days when I don't understand.*

dream a little dream

# Sweep Away the Rubbish

*"Love never stops being patient, never stops believing, never stops hoping, never gives up."*
—1 Corinthians 13:7

Finally! After years of fixing up other people's old houses, a new home is being built just for us. I am excited envisioning our masterpiece of a house—everything perfect, freshly painted, and never dirtied. I dream of bathing in a sparkling clean, never-used bathtub. I yearn for the day I can put my dishes in sanitized cupboards not mysteriously stained by a previous owner's unknown food or bloodied finger. With anticipation and hope, we make nightly visits to see what wonders the carpenter has performed that day.

What disappointment! What a mess! Rubbish consisting of pieces of cement, nails, half-filled Styrofoam coffee cups, and half-smoked cigarette butts litter my floor. The entire home, including those never-bloodied cupboards and never-bathed-in bathtubs, is dirty with layers of fine spackle dust. Endless delays and setbacks produce daily testing of my patience. Nonetheless, I refuse to be discouraged by all the disappointments of the ongoing construction. Realizing house building is dirty business, my mind sweeps away the rubbish and imagines the beauty of the completed home.

We need to do the same as God constructs our children. In the growing process, there is a lot of rubbish. Disappointments, messy rooms, bloody noses, wild hairdos, tattoos, and hidden cigarette butts are construction problems which can blur our eyes and cloud our judgment. Each of these setbacks demands so much attention and patience that we can lose sight of the Master Carpenter.

God isn't finished with His construction of our children. He keeps sawing, hammering, and completing the work He began. We need to keep our mind's eye not on the sawdust but on the beautiful creation God is forming into an adult. Don't let the rubbish get you down. Sweep it away, enjoy your children, and expect a completed masterpiece.

*Lord Jesus, You are the Master Builder of my children. You aren't finished with them yet. Why, You aren't even finished with me yet! Help me keep my eyes and thoughts on You as the Master Carpenter and the completed masterpiece and not on all the mess along the way. Love always hopes. I love and, therefore, I hope. Thank You, Jesus, for the hope I have in You.*

# Stirring the Pot

*"Hate starts quarrels, but love covers every wrong."*
—Proverbs 10:12

"Reservations!" may be our favorite dinner entree, but we all spend some time at our stoves. Whether we cook often or seldom, it is good to take a peak at who is stirring our pots—Hatred or Love?

Hatred stands at her stove stirring the pot. She becomes more furious and vicious as each swipe of the spoon brings up past pain and injury. Hatred keeps stirring to make sure she doesn't miss any of the ugliest memories. While scraping the bottom of the pot, she delights in the dissension she discovers she has almost forgotten, but even that is not enough. Hatred knows just what buttons to push to turn up the heat. She makes the fire hotter and hotter. The contents of the pot swell, getting bigger and bubblier. Frantically, Hatred keeps stirring and turning up the heat. Soon, the pot is overflowing and spewing dissension over the top of the stove. She realizes too late that the stove is a mess and so is her marriage. The hot liquid is uncontrollably overflowing. It begins its deadly descent spilling off the stove, scarring the scalps and minds of her innocent little children playing at her side.

Love views her pot much differently. Noticing the wrongs brewing inside, she quickly takes the lid and covers the pot. Love refuses to lift the lid fearing any forgiven and forgotten dissension may sneak out. She decides it is best not to push the buttons and turn up the heat. Love is sometimes tempted to peak into the pot but stops herself and determines, "No, I'm not going there. I won't look in that pot." Love discerns the difference between brewing problems that need a little stir and those minor irritations that are better left covered. After much sacrifice, her stove is clean, her marriage content, and her little children play happily on the floor at her side.

If we aren't happy with the person stirring our pot, it's not too late to replace the cook. Who stands at our stove, what buttons are pushed, and how frantically we beat are the decisions we make every day. Certainly, there are times when our pot needs a good stir. We shouldn't put the lid on big problems. But there are other moments when the little, unimportant irritations are better left covered.

King Solomon states in Proverbs 10:12, "Hatred stirs up dissension, but love covers over all wrongs" (NIV). Solomon never placed a foot in our homes, but he knew that some days Hatred would stir, and on others, Love would cover. May we choose our battles with the wisdom of Solomon. May God give us wisdom to know when to stir the pot and when to leave the lid on. Our families will then play safely without fear of the person named Hatred.

*Lord, I know there are times when I need to lovingly confront and communicate. Big problems should not be left under cover. However, there are so many times when the little, unimportant irritations swell, and I can be so quick to stir the pot. May I be a woman named Love. Give me godly wisdom to know when to uncover the pot and when to keep the lid on. Please keep my heart and my stove clean. Protect my marriage and my children from me. Thank You, Jesus.*

# Singing in the Shower

*"Then our mouths were filled with laughter and our tongues with joyful songs."*

–Psalm 126:2a

If every day is a gift, why aren't we having a party? Our children would love each day to be a celebration. Two-year-old Sam rises with the sun in eager anticipation of the new day. "Get up everybody! The sun's out! It's going to be a beautiful day!" He exclaims even throughout dreary March. Sam's joy of living is contagious.

Our family catches Sam's enthusiasm. Joanna, the practical joker, squeals in delight as she pours a pitcher of cold water over her unsuspecting sister singing in the shower. Dumping dog food into the Wheaties and watching our sleepy eyes miss it as our mouths eat it is another of Joanna's amusements. Sweet Elizabeth's fun isn't in playing practical jokes. We call her "Birdie" for all the melodious tunes she sings throughout the day. The laughter and the songs fill our home with joy.

*"All right, Susie Sunshine,"* you're thinking, *"every day is not a party. Some days I find no balloons, and I grow tired of picking up confetti. I can't celebrate every day. Someone has to do the work."* True, but why not party while we work? What do we have to lose? Rejoice as we clean our children's rooms. Fill the air with laughter as we sweep and dust and gag at locker room smells. When the laundry has us buried, let's bury our children in prayer. Every little sock tucked into a nursery drawer can represent a blessing for our little ones. Work and life are much sweeter when a song and prayer fill the air.

We all need showers. While we're wet, we might as well start singing. If we're blessed, we might get a pitcher of cold water lovingly poured on our head. I suspect if we sing loudly enough even the dog will join us in a robust chorus. Get grumpy and see how quickly our homes are filled with gloom. It's our choice. Let's choose Sam's way. Decide to clap our hands and sing "Oh what a beautiful morning!" even on cloudy days.

Life is short. Let's make it an event to remember.

*Oh Lord, I need to do some singing. Please cleanse my heart of a critical, bitter, discontent, and unhappy spirit. Fill me with songs of praise to You for the family You have given me. May they hear love in my laughter and a prayer in my song.*

# Glennora

*"Imitate God, since you are the children he loves. Live in love as Christ also loved us. He gave his life for us as an offering and sacrifice, a soothing aroma to God."*

—Ephesians 5:1-2

Squeezing the last drip out of the toothpaste tube, I proudly announce two more weeks of brushing were realized from the not-quite-empty tube my husband had thrown away fourteen days before. My beloved smiles and affectionately calls me, "Glennora." Glennora is what Dan lovingly calls me when I remind him of my dear dad, Glenn. My father would have still gotten another two weeks out of that tube of toothpaste. He was a master at saving a penny. Proudly, I am very much like my dad, and although unintentionally, I have picked up many of my father's mannerisms.

Our children will imitate us. We capture hints of our own clunky walk as our child struts across the school stage receiving a reading award. We grimace at the walk and grin at the award. Our love for books is being imitated, too. How proud we are when our children imitate our good habits. How horrifying when they imitate habits we wish we had been rid of years ago.

Scripture says we are to be "imitators of God" and to "live a life of love" (Ephesians 5:1-2 NIV). Living a life of love is easily understood but not so easily imitated. Do we love the unlovely, both our enemies and our neighbors? Do we forgive as God forgave us? Do we show God's mercy and love to all people?

To imitate God and live a life of love requires we give ourselves up. I suspect we don't imitate God because we aren't willing to give ourselves up. We are selfish. We want things our way, not God's way. Morally questionable television shows lure us. There's more time for the morning newspaper than morning prayer. It feels good to sleep in on Sunday morning and miss time with the One who gave us the day in the first place. I think we get the picture. Our lives are to be a photo copy of Jesus, who gave Himself up for us. This is truly the life of love we want our children to see in us and imitate.

Our children are watching us. If they'll simulate the process of eliminating the toothpaste, I know they'll copy other areas of our lives as well. As we imitate God, and our children imitate us, we'll be doing much less grimacing and much more grinning.

*Lord, look in my heart and show me areas in my life where I do not imitate You. Cleanse me of any activity or thought which does not reflect Your holiness. My children are watching me. May they see Christ in me. If I am to imitate You, I must know You. Help me to know You more by daily studying Your Word and communicating to You through prayer. Thank You for Your forgiveness and mercy. May I show the same to my children as I live a life of love and self-sacrifice. Thank You, Jesus, for being worthy of imitation.*

# Don't Stop Loving Me

*"Love never stops being patient, never stops believing, never stops hoping, never gives up."*
—1 Corinthians 13:7

Placed on the chair for a "time out" the weepy two year old wonders why he misbehaves as he whimpers, "I be a good boy." In his heart, he is persevering at being good while we are certain he is mastering being bad. All the while, his defiant heart is crying out, "Don't stop loving me! Don't give up on me!" Who can understand a two year old?

God can. He understands children, and He understands mothers as well. God is aware of the problems pummeling our homes requiring patience and perseverance. That is why His definition of love begins with the word *patience* and ends with the word *perseveres*—or "never gives up." God knows our children will exasperate our patience, and He exhorts us to persevere in loving our children through all of the difficult times. We must never give up our efforts to mother, and we must never give up loving our children. They are crying out to us to love them the way God intended, the way God loves us.

In God's definition of love, He places the word *always* before the word *perseveres*. We are not given a choice. No matter the trouble, we are to always persevere. Webster defines perseverance as "to continue in some effort, course of action...in spite of difficulty, opposition... be steadfast in purpose; persist." We are to "always" persist and be steadfast in purpose. We are to always love. We are never to give up on ourselves or our children.

God is our example of perfect love. How often we exasperate Him, disappoint Him, and wrong Him, yet He never gives up on us. He never withdraws His love from us. He is patient and always perseveres. We must do the same for our children. Never give up on them. Never stop loving them.

*Lord, some days are hard and long. Help me to love my children the way You love me. You never give up on me. You never stop loving me even when I displease You. Give me a great dose of patience. May I never be tempted to give up on my children or to think You have given up on them. May I be steadfast in purpose in spite of difficulty or opposition. You, Jesus, have loved me through all the times I have disappointed You. Thank You for my "time outs" and Your hugs once my discipline is over. You are a loving, patient, and persevering God. May I be like You.*

# The Passing Storm

*"You have changed my sobbing into dancing. You have removed my sackcloth and clothed me with joy so that my soul may praise you with music and not be silent."*

—Psalm 30:11–12a

They were thankful for the thunder and lightning. It synchronized with the storm raging in their hearts. The loud thunderclap drowned their voices as they cried out to God, "How could you let this happen?"

They had planned their lives perfectly, both working and saving to buy the big house they would fill with children. Dancing in the large, childless home, they celebrated and anticipated their first child. Soon, their dancing turned to wailing at the news their little daughter needed heart surgery, and their prayers to have more children appeared to go unanswered. They resolved that their dreams were not God's plans or His timing.

God planned the storm, and He provided peace and calm in the eye of it. His comforting presence assured them that the storm in their hearts, like the one in the sky, would pass. Seeking God, they opened their Bibles and read James 1:27: "Religion that God our Father accepts as pure and faultless is this: to look after orphans..." (NIV). "That's it!" proclaimed the new daddy, "We'll fill this house with orphans."

Their wailing became a continuous dance as foster children pranced into their lives. One, then three, finally, four toddlers skipped merrily into the large house God knew they would need. It wasn't long before they realized being foster parents was not working for them. With their hearts filled with love, they gave all four children their last name on adoption papers, and their daughter with the heart problem even now grows strong and tall and laughs merrily as she leads her younger siblings in a jig. One wonders where these little children would be if God had blessed this family with only sunny days.

*Dear Jesus, thank you for thunderstorms in my life. Remind me to seek You in the midst of them. You have brought the bad weather for a purpose: to clean me and conform me to Your plan. May I trust You as You lead me through the storms of life. You will turn my wailing into a dance and clothe me with joy. May I be patient and careful not to step on Your toes as we dance through life together.*

# Rare and Well Done

*"There are different types of work to do, but the same God produces every gift in every person."*
—1 Corinthians 12:6

While sitting by the lake, I observe a smorgasbord of life. Children, wearing sun protection, play in the warm sand. Teens, wearing very little, tan on beach blankets. Grandparents, wearing hats, seek protection from the sun under beach umbrellas. Parents, wearing the weight of the world, commingle among the generations somewhere between the warm sand and the beach umbrellas. Such a mix of people with Jesus working in all of them.

Not every day is like a day at the beach. Daily life delivers what some may call "pot luck." Each day is a mystery stew of good and bad, heartache and joy. Until you dig in, you aren't quite sure if "Today's Special" will be bitter or sweet. Life deals a variety of days to people in all crawls, walks, and limps of life. But this we know, Jesus is working in all of their lives.

Each day and each person are created by God to be different than the one made the day before. Why are we so surprised when children from the same family are so opposite? One child may be too zealous for life, and we wish he would calm down. The other seems too placid, and we wonder why she isn't more enthusiastic. One's non-stop questions are so tiring, yet another child's quietness has us concerned. Our children are all different. We can't order them "rare" or "well done." We take them as God gives them to us.

Children seem like a mystery stew to us, but God knows all about them, and He has great plans for their day. He likes them "rare," for He creates each one uniquely. He assures us they are "well done" because He created them in the image of the Almighty God who does all things well. The world is filled with different personalities given by God for the variety of work to be done in the kingdom. Let's not carry the weight of the world on our shoulders. The Master Chef is at work, and the stew isn't a mystery to Him.

*Lord, thank You for creating my children "rare." There are no others like them. May I enjoy my children and encourage them to be all that You created them to be. Thank You that they are all "well done." You created them in Your image, and you can't get "weller" than that! Each child and each day are made by You different than the ones before. You are at work in me, in my children, and in my day. Cleanse my heart from trying to interfere with Your job. May I trust You as You work and I enjoy the picnic on the beach.*

# Finding Your Patience Before You Lose It

*"But the spiritual nature produces love, joy, peace, patience, kindness, goodness, faithfulness, gentleness, and self-control."*

—Galatians 5:22–23a

Patience. Where do we leave it when we lose it? A little boy may have been searching for his mother's patience on the beach. He was so excited, that he cried out, "Mommy, Mommy, Mommy, look what I found!" She barked her response, "I wish you would stop calling 'Mommy!' I can't stand it! I just need a break!" Somewhere in the sand, her patience was lost.

We mothers know the sadness in our children's eyes when we find our patience missing. We desperately need to locate it before permanent scars are engraved upon the hearts of our little ones because they believe every impatient word spoken. We love our children. We don't want to harm them with words.

So, why is patience so often lost? Living with children is not easy. Mothering is tiring business, and when we grow tired, we become impatient. Tempers flare as a warning that a self-examination and a time-evaluation are needed.

Asking ourselves some simple questions and changing our lifestyles may help us find our patience before it is lost again. Are we getting enough rest? Are our tired bodies getting proper nutrition and exercise? Do we need to say "no" to some of the demands on our lives outside the home? Is it time for a night out or a weekend away with our husband? When did we last spend time resting in the patient arms of Jesus?

Patience is a fruit of God's Spirit. If we seek Jesus, we'll find our patience. As we remain in the branches of His fruit tree, we'll never find it missing again. It was there all the time.

*Lord, I can't do this in my own strength. I pray for patience that comes from You. Protect me from the busyness and exhaustion of this life. I want to be like You, for You never lost your patience, and You never hurried anywhere. I ask that Your patience reside in my heart and control me. Thank You for being patient and loving with me. I love you, Jesus.*

# Challenging a Challenging Child

*"I know the plans that I have for you, declares the Lord. They are plans for peace and not disaster, plans to give you a future filled with hope."*

—Jeremiah 29:11

He was the terror of the Sunday School. All of the teachers shuddered at thoughts of this disruptive boy being promoted into their Sunday School class. All but one. She didn't tremble at his misbehavior; she observed his character. Studying him, she noted he had an exceptionally bright mind, a quick wit, and an incredible memory. She challenged this challenging boy to memorize scripture. He did. No longer a loser, he won scripture memory awards and free trips to scripture memory summer camps. Today, he is a pastor noted for his quiet, gentle spirit. He uses his bright mind, quick wit, and incredible memory to serve the Lord. God had a plan, a hope, and a future for the terror of the Sunday School.

Mothers of Sunday School terrors can feel hopeless. The despair of raising challenging children can blind our eyes to the good qualities God has placed in each child. However, sometimes there is just no energy left in our tired bodies to focus on anything but our own fatigue.

During these "end-of-my-rope" moments, we need to wake up and attack. But first, we need to prepare for battle. Arm yourself with pen and paper. Choose the right time for the confrontation, preferably when your little demon looks more like an angel. I suggest while the child is sleeping. Focus on your child and write every good character trait and ability you have ever seen in your little or big one. Read it often. Display it for all to see. Add to the list as years go by. As you and your challenging child focus more on good qualities than bad, everyone will be surprised at the positive changes. And, I expect, you'll be winning more of the challenges.

*Dear Jesus, I pray I will see my children through Your eyes. You have a plan, a hope, and a future for them. Keep me from focusing on what they do wrong and help me see their good, their gifts, and their talents. Cleanse my heart of defeat and fill it with hope. Please give me wisdom and strength. Thank You for being patient with me when I am Your challenging child. You forgive my faults and focus on my potential. Help me do the same with my children.*

# White House—Green Trim

*"Life is not about having a lot of material possessions."*
—Luke 12:15b

Today I walked out of my childhood home for the last time. My parents are selling the property they purchased forty-one years ago, a month before I was born. The real estate agent listed the house as a "two bedroom bungalow." She had no clue of the property's value or the priceless love that indwells it. My eyes fill with tears, and my heart fills with memories as I recall growing up in the white house with green trim.

I didn't have a bedroom, only a mattress with a small chest of drawers at the top of the stairs. My brothers snored in the cubicle next to me, and a sister slept in the room on the other side. Parents and baby sister occupied the bedroom below. In more ways than one, I was the middle child. It was great. I could spy on everybody. Six children were tucked in nice and cozy.

The realtor must have been amused at thoughts of the brood raised here. If so, the newspaper made no reference to it. The ad only talked of wood frames, room size, and a new furnace. There was no mention of the things that really kept us warm.

The maple tree under which Mom and Dad cooled themselves on hot days wasn't thought of as an asset. I received hours of therapy swinging and singing from that huge tree. On a good swing, I could touch the leaves with my toes as God touched my life with His peace. The yard was perfect for bare feet and baseball and hide-and-go-seek. Well, maybe not hide-and-go-seek. My brothers always made sure I was "it." That probably wouldn't be a selling point.

It is likely that no one would be interested in the chicken coop. Maybe they'll let me keep it in the deal. I raised chickens in that coop. It was horrible when I was expected to eat my pals for Sunday dinner. Everyone filled their tummies with my chickens while I filled my plate with tears. When the chickens were gone, the coop became my lovely playhouse shadowed by the beautiful cherry tree. It was its own retreat center complete with springtime blossoms and summertime breakfast, lunch, and dinner. Perhaps the chicken coop and cherry tree were listed separately. Although, I doubt many would be attracted to such a sanctuary.

I grew up in a day when God's nature was my playground. My life was full, and my possessions were few. Today some parents fear their children won't know what love is unless they have their own room complete with bathroom, telephone, TV, and computer. In the midst of our desire to "provide adequately" for our children, we may be denying them peaceful, character-building pleasures. I heard once, "You can spoil your children with material goods, but you will never spoil them with love." There is nothing wrong with giving our children the best our money can buy, but in the process, let us not forget the free fun found in maple trees, chicken coops, and cherry breakfasts.

*Lord, thank You for the wonderful playground You have provided for my children. May they see that fun doesn't have to be man-made with a price tag. I pray they will know the joy of bare feet and tall grass, maple tree swings, and cherry tree treats. Fill my home with love, good memories, and Christ. His home is never listed with a realtor. He will never leave us nor change. Thank You for that stability. Thank You for residing in cherry trees, chicken coops, and two-bedroom bungalows. Thank You for living in my heart.*

# Proud Parenting

*"[Love] doesn't sing it own praises."*
—1 Corinthians 13:4b

We're exhausted! We've rushed little Billy to soccer and hurried him to his Little League game. Oh dear, if the game goes too long, we'll have to pull him out so he won't be late for his piano recital. Why, he is so fluent in French, that we've been advised to hire a tutor!

We hurry our children here, there, and everywhere so they can learn everything and be accelerated, and we can be so proud of them. Let's pause a moment to ask ourselves a question. Are we really proud of them, or are we proud of our own endeavors to be an exhausted parent? When we rush our children trying to give them the best of life, we can deprive them of their own childhood. Activities are beneficial for children but not if the only memory they create is a frazzled mother screaming, "Hurry up!"

My mother never hurried me to the cherry tree. I ran there without any coaxing or activity fees. I don't recall her boasting to her friends about all the hours I spent lying in that big tree. One branch was so wide I could safely lie on my back, look through the green leaves to the blue sky, and eat a tummy full of cherries. I did my best thinking and learning in that cherry tree. I talked to God, and He talked to me. I listened to birds and watched clouds turn into animals in the sky. Nobody rushed me. I was enjoying being a child.

Adulthood comes much too quickly. Let's not rush our children to experience its pace, and let's especially not hurry our children for the sole purpose of the fulfillment it brings us in boasting about it. Remember, quiet times and a simple life can be our children's best teacher.

*Dear Jesus, I am tired of running this parenting race. I am weary of keeping up with everyone's goal to raise accomplished children. May I give my children memories of happiness not hecticness. May they know more about serenity than schedules. May we not be so busy playing the world's games that we miss Your beautiful creation. Help me to remember You are the best tutor, and time with You is priceless. Thank You, Jesus, for this reminder to love my children and let them enjoy their wonderful childhood years.*

# It was the Worst of Times—
# It was the Best of Times

*"We know that all things work together for the good of those who love God—those whom he has called according to his plan."*

—Romans 8:28

This was only his second Christmas, and it was to be his last. My baby brother's cancer was diagnosed when he was nine months old. Six months to live was the hope we were given. A God who answers prayer was the hope to which we clung. It was the worst of times.

For nine months, we had enjoyed this special gift from God given as a caboose on a train of six. His older siblings doted on him, and he filled our home with a new baby's joy, lots of laughter and lullabies and "peek-a-boos." We believed the future was bright. It was the best of times.

Then, suddenly and shockingly, the news hit us. We watched in horror as our bouncing baby brother suffered the effects of surgeries and radiation. Now thin, sickly, and strapped immobile in his hospital bed, his faint smile broke our already broken hearts.

My mother ached at the expected loss of her youngest child. Rising early for the long drive to Children's Hospital, spending the day loving her suffering little son, and coming home late and exhausted became her routine. It amazed me she had the strength to cry night after night. I am sure she grieved not just the loss of her baby but the time lost with her children at home. How were they doing in school? How were they coping with this pain? This is not what any mother wishes for her child, be that child nine months or sixteen years.

I hurt. I suffered the pain of losing my sweet baby brother and listening to my mother cry. My teenagehood was interrupted. While my friends were busy with hairdos and proms and college applications, I was thinking about the importance of family, the brevity of life, and the preciousness of each day.

My life changed at age sixteen. A bad hair day no longer meant the world was ending. Spending time with my family was more momentous than going to the prom. Wanting to do something meaningful with my life replaced any desire to make lots of money. People became more important than possessions.

Looking back now, I realize the blessings of this experience. What would I be like today if I had been spared this suffering? I suspect shallower, less compassionate, not as fulfilled or as happy. God used the worst time of my life, and eventually, it became the best thing that ever happened to me. My life has been better because of the pain.

And the best is last: God performed a miracle. My brother lives! He has celebrated forty Christmases and plans to enjoy many more.

*Lord, no mother wants to see her children in pain. It is our natural instinct to protect our young. Help me as a mom realize that I can't shelter my children from the difficulties of life. Let me trust You to work and mold my children for good. When trials come, keep me strong as I keep my eyes on You and not on the pain. When it is the worst of times, help me remember You will eventually make it the best of times. May I wait patiently for You to complete the work and teach all the lessons. I look forward to the good that will come from every trial.*

# God Owns It All

*"Everything under heaven belongs to me."*

—Job 41:11b

"Mine!" asserts the two year old proudly proclaiming his rights to a toy taken by a brother. Sadly, *mine* is one of the first words spoken. We don't teach children to be selfish. They are born this way.

"God owns it all!" is printed across the checkbook cover of a mother who has learned to trust God for His provision. What a contrast! Somewhere between toddlerhood and adulthood she forfeited her rights to God. She learned it was God who said, "Everything under heaven belongs to me." Too many of us think we penned that phrase.

Will the two year old one day surrender ownership not only of his toys but of his life? Have we? Could we print "God owns it all" across our checkbook? Our toys? Our children? If God took our dearest possession away, would we be all right knowing it was never ours anyway? Forfeiting our rights to our toys and our checkbook is one thing. Giving our children back to God is quite another. I suspect a mother's greatest fear (or close to it) is losing a child.

Sitting with a grieving mother at the bedside of her dying son, I sense God is sitting with us, too. Accepting reality, the mother whispers, "He isn't mine. He belongs to God." She watches as her precious little baby slips into the arms of Jesus, and Jesus slips His strong arms of comfort around her. Peace that passes understanding fills her heart. Her son is with his real owner. She knows it is all right even if she doesn't understand why.

*Lord, cleanse my heart of thoughts that anything belongs to me. May I mentally stamp "God owns it all" across everything I claim as mine. Thank you for my children. I know they really belong to You, and You can take them back at any moment. May I not live in fear of that truth but in trust. You assure me that if the worst happens Your arms will carry me through difficult days.*

*Thank You for my checkbook. On days when it is full, I seek Your will in distribution of Your money. On days when it is empty, I thank You for Your provision to meet all my needs.*

*Thank You for my toys. I enjoy them. May I not be selfish with these gifts nor envious of others' abundance.*

*Thank You for my life. May I live each day knowing it is a gift from You. I surrender my life to You, Jesus. Everything under heaven belongs to you. There couldn't be a better owner and that brings me peace.*

# Cheek-to-Cheek

*"Flesh and blood give birth to flesh and blood, but the Spirit gives birth to things that are spiritual."*
—John 3:6

Words fail the feelings in my heart as I anticipate the arrival of my first-born child. Not as eager to greet me, she enjoys her peace and rest in the solace of my womb. I sing to her, talk to her, and jokingly name her "Hank." She is so loved and wanted in my life.

Her stubbornness showing even in her birth, she lingers too long and fights the muscles miraculously working to bring her from my womb into my arms. Hands strapped to my sides in preparation for an emergency C-section, I am thankful to be kept awake and alert. I don't want to miss any of her life. Her first cry brings big tears of joy and relief to me. Unable to move, I plead to see her and to touch this miracle. My arms ache more from desire to put my child in my arms than from the operating table restraints.

A faceless nurse brings still-crying Joanna to me and places our faces cheek-to-cheek. Our tears melt into one as a final farewell to our oneness. I smile and speak a simple, "I love you, Joanna." Her crying immediately stops as she hears the familiar voice of her mother. We are bonded forever. I long to dance through life with her cheek-to-cheek. To never leave her. To always assure her of my love. To share every tear and celebrate every joy.

God is like this. He desires to go dancing through life with us cheek-to-cheek, our tears melting with His. He is always eager to say, "I love you, my child." How often we resist Him as we seek every road and piece of advice but His. We don't want to be born into His kingdom. We like it in our worldly womb. All the while, He is calling us to Himself, waiting for us to stop struggling in our own strength and to come to Him. He longs to hold us, comfort us, and help us through life's joys and trials. He is our "Abba"—Daddy, and He wants the first dance.

*Oh Lord, I remember the joy of holding my first-born child. Remind me that you experience the same joy when I rest in Your arms. I don't want to dance through life without you. Let us go cheek-to-cheek together and let me always follow your lead.*

because his mercy endures forever.

because his mercy endures forever.

because his mercy endures forever.

...remembered us when we were humiliated—
    because his mercy endures forever.
...ched us from the grasp of our enemies—
    because his mercy endures forever.
...gives food to every living creature—
    because his mercy endures forever.
...ve thanks to the God of heaven
    because his mercy endures forever.

## Psalm 137

By the rivers of Babylon, we sat down and cried
    as we remembered Zion.
We hung our lyres on willow trees.
It was there that those who had captured us demanded that we sing.
    Those who guarded us wanted us to entertain them.
    They said, "Sing a song from Zion for us!"

How could we sing the Lord's song in a foreign land?
If I forget you, Jerusalem,
    let my right hand forget how to play the lyre.
Let my tongue stick to the roof of my m...
    if I don't remember you,
    if I don't consider Jerusale...

O Lord, remember the pe...
    Remember what the...
    They said, "Tea...
You destructive pe...
    blessed is the...
    with the...
Blessed is...
    and sm...

# A Wake-Up Call

*"This is what the Lord says: 'Don't be afraid, my servant Jacob, Jeshurun, whom I have chosen. I will pour water on thirsty ground and rain on dry land. I will pour my Spirit on your offspring and my blessing on your descendants. They will spring up with the grass as poplars spring up by streams.'"*

—Isaiah 44:2b–4

The radio alarm goes off on time, 6:00 A.M. The weatherman's familiar voice nudges me awake. He assures me of blue skies today. *That's nice*, I think, somewhat soothed. Blue skies are outside, but inside I feel a bit gray. It is moving day, and I am apprehensive of what lies ahead. How sad I feel about leaving friends, how excited to meet new ones. A new home to decorate, new neighborhoods to explore, new stores to discover. I fear I'm too old for all this newness.

Then I remember my children. What will this move do to them? They are at an impressionable age. Will they adjust? Will their grades go down? They are so good here. What if they hate it there? I wish they weren't facing new friends with unknown reputations who may lead them down dead-end roads or worse. My heart is as heavy as the packed boxes surrounding me.

I then spy my friend, the Bible, on top of one of the boxes. If ever there were a day I am too busy for morning devotions, it is today. If ever there were a day I need God, it is today. "Just give me something to hold onto, Lord. Today, when my whole life is moving, I need stability from You." I whisper a prayer as I randomly open His Word. My eyes fall on Isaiah 44: "Do not be afraid…I will pour out my Spirit on your offspring, and my blessing on your descendants. They will spring up like grass in a meadow, like poplar trees by flowing streams" (2b–3 NIV).

"Oh, thank You, Lord! You have assured me my children will grow and thrive even in this new, unknown place." In the early morning, God gives me a "wake-up" call. How those words minister to my fear-filled heart on that moving day and for many days to follow! My children will be all right. God promised me.

I wonder. How many times do we leave time with God out of our day and miss a very special word He has for us? I wonder what needless anxiety we experience because we let the weatherman wake us up instead of God.

*Lord, thank You for never being too busy for me. May I never be too busy for You. You are my dearest friend. Thank You for never moving from me. May I never move from You. Oh, what blessings I miss when I don't walk with You and talk with you. Don't let me begin a day without You. Let us wake up and begin each day together. Thank you, Jesus.*

# Let Your Imagination Run Wild

*"Glory belongs to God, whose power is at work in us. By this power he can do infinitely more than we can ask or imagine."*

—Ephesians 3:20

The news hit the young mother like a baseball hurled hard into her heart. Her newborn has cystic fibrosis. No warning. No preparation. Just present pain and future fear. Her world is suddenly surrounded with doctors, nurses, needles, hospitals, and a baby laboring to breathe. No promises other than the promise that her life will change. It will be difficult because her child's existence could end suddenly and soon. Comforting friends, unable to comfort, bring meals, hugs, and prayers.

God has never left her, yet she senses His arrival. His peaceful presence envelopes her with hope as she takes her eyes off of the cystic fibrosis and focuses on the God who created her precious child in His image. He whispers into her heart the familiar words, "I can do more than you can ask or imagine."

"Wow! I've always had a wild imagination! I can imagine a lot! I see my son kicking a soccer ball for the goal and running all the bases with breath to spare! I imagine him growing into a great man of God who serves Him with all his heart and proclaims Him with every breath. And God says He will do even more than I can imagine!" She smiles at the thought of this bright future. With God's help, she imagines great things for her baby and refuses to allow anything to destroy her hope and joy. She now comforts her son with the promise she has received from God and entertains him with her wild imagination.

*Lord, there are days I feel so overwhelmed with despair. Cleanse my heart of hopelessness and fill it with faith. May I keep my eyes fixed on You who can do immeasurably more than all I ask or imagine. Give me a wild imagination and a generous portion of patience and trust as You work.*

# I Want It My Way

*"My thoughts are not your thoughts, and my ways are not your ways,' declares the Lord."*

—Isaiah 55:8

We have it all figured out, don't we? We'll do everything right, and our children will do everything right, and we'll all live happily ever after. Fairy tales give mothers false hope. Babies are only days old before we realize we don't have a clue what "do everything right" means.

Nevertheless, we do our best to teach our children the way we think they should go and how we expect things to be done. We tell them with our lives and disciplinary tactics, "I want you to do it my way." Our babies arch their little backs and try to assert their independence. Usually, mom wins, and children learn life is easier if they do it mom's way. All the while, they make mental notes of big plans once they are away from mother's eyesight.

A rebellious child can break a mother's heart. Ejected from college, a son must now make his own way, a route more difficult that his mother hoped he would avoid. Disobedience leads him down hard and lonely roads. Nevertheless, God is with him. The Heavenly Father teaches him and grows him into the man He intended him to be. God's ways were different than the mother's ways. God chose an alternate passage for her son, a trail where the son would learn to help lost people find their way. God's path led this man through many battles and finally into God's army.

We mothers would choose only smooth roads for our children. We panic watching our children choose bumpy, dangerous routes, but God's ways are better than our ways. The bumpy byway may be in His plan to teach the lessons that a smooth road could not teach.

*S.O.S. Dear Lord, I've cleared a perfect path for my children. When they choose to cut their own way, please protect them from the weeds. Increase my faith to trust You that Your hand is leading them for Your purpose. How much better Your ways are than mine. Thank You, Jesus, that I can entrust my children to You.*

# Morning Cuddles

*"In the morning, O Lord, hear my voice. In the morning I lay my needs in front of you, and I wait."*
—Psalm 5:3

"Morning Cuddles, Mommy!" pleaded three little ones in unison coming to me with thumb in mouth and favorite blanket or stuffed animal dragging on the floor behind them. Before they sought anything else, they sought me. We cuddled up in my bed, sang songs, read a book or two, laughed a lot, tickled each other's tummies, made big plans for the day, and prayed to God—not necessarily in that order. My children hugged me tightly never wanting to let me go until they had sufficient cuddles. It was therapeutic for all of us. What a wonderful way to begin the day!

As they grew and school books replaced stuffed bears, we continued to enjoy our morning cuddles. A little more hurried now as devotional books were read while cereal was slurped. Prayers and hugs happened in a rush not to miss the school bus. Still, it was a precious time. They wouldn't step outside until they were covered by their mother's arms and prayers. It made us feel good, and I imagine that it made God feel good, too.

God is very willing to have "morning cuddles." He'll wrap His strong arms around us, share His Book, and sing to our hearts. When we don't have morning cuddles with God, I suspect He misses that time with us. I know we miss that time with Him. We shouldn't take one step in our day without His loving arms and prayers covering us. Before we seek anything else, we should seek Him. It is a wonderful way to begin the day!

*Dear Lord, thank You that You are always there to cuddle me, laugh and cry with me, help me, guide me, and strengthen me. You know what I will need each day. May I seek You before I seek anything else.*

# The Over-Protective Parent

*"[Love] isn't happy when injustice is done, but it is happy with the truth. Love never stops being patient, never stops believing, never stops hoping, never gives up."*

—1 Corinthians 13:6–7

The first step, first overnight, first day of school, first date, graduation, college, and marriage—all represent momentous occasions which can wreak havoc on our emotions as we lose control of our children. We would love to keep them in our care, protected forever from bad decisions, bad drivers, and bad friends. It won't happen. We can't follow them around for the rest of their lives foreseeing, hovering, and protecting them from trouble. Even the most protected child can slip onto the wrong path in a moment. We are helpless, but we aren't hopeless.

Prayer is the best protection we can give our children. How comforting for children to know there is a God who loves, cares, and hears a mother's prayers for them. Leaving the house each day, my children waited, seemingly hesitant to enter the world without prayers of protection. "Aren't you going to pray?" they would ask, standing at the backdoor. The anxiety of being late for school was less than the apprehension of going into an unknown day without their mother's prayers. They felt safe walking out the door knowing their mother was praying and God was protecting.

Today, I still receive telephone calls from my grown children asking for my continued prayers. They need their independence, and I am careful not to interfere, but I am pleased that they yearn for my continued intercession. Could a parent have a more important responsibility? Could a child feel more loved and protected?

We will not always go where our children go, but we can pray, and God will go and protect them.

*Keep me on my knees, Lord, as my children grow and become independent. Thank You for protecting them along their way. Thank You for your angels of protection hovering around them and keeping them safe. When bad things happen to them, help me to trust that You are still protecting them. Sometimes I feel helpless, but I am never hopeless. I know You are with them, loving, caring, and protecting them in ways I can't even see. Thank You, dear Jesus.*

# An A+ in Parenting

*"I look up toward the mountains. Where can I find help?"*

—Psalm 121:1

If ever there is a test we want to ace, it is our parenting exam. When I became a mom, I wanted to get an A+ in parenting, so I studied. I filled my bookcases, heart, and head with information on how to parent. There are, more or less, 26,000 books written on this subject, each touting its own method of child rearing. While gaining some good advice, I feared my parenting books were like my dieting books, each promising success but not delivering results.

Where is a mother to turn? These authors aren't perfect parents, and they never met my children. How could they know the right way to raise my unique gift from God? One day the answer came to me. I was looking for parenting help from every source except the One who knew my children best—their Creator.

*"Aha!"* I realized, *"God knit my babies in my womb. He knows my children intimately.* What they are thinking and how they feel every minute of every day is no mystery to God. He knows why they misbehave. He knows their needs, their fears, and their joys. He is the only perfect parent, and He loves them even more than I can. And God has written a book! It's a best seller! The Bible is the perfect parenting book because it was written by the only perfect parent.

God didn't knit our children and then leave us to figure out the rest. He didn't wash His hands and say, "Well, I've done my part. Nice looking baby, there! My work is finished." No, God loves and cares for mothers and their babies long after delivery day.

When my daughter, Joanna, was a teenager she informed me, "I really have three parents: mom, dad, and God. You and dad can't always be with me, but God never leaves me, so I am never without a parent." It is comforting to know the parent who is omnipresent is the one who never misses an answer on a parenting test.

In our parenting course, the best teacher is our Heavenly Father and the perfect textbook is the Bible. God has also provided us with the most effective parenting tool—prayer. God hears mothers' prayers and answers them with wisdom and strength. He is available twenty four hours a day, and He never grows weary of us talking about our children. We need to ask Him to help us raise them.

I so wanted to be an A+ mom, but I failed. We all fail. We are imperfect parents raising imperfect children in an imperfect world. But we have not been left to do it alone. We have a teacher whose door is always open. We have a textbook with every answer. We have access to the only perfect parent, our Heavenly Father. He's waiting and wanting to hear from us. God loves it when we seek His guidance, and He wants to help us raise kids who love Him.

*Thank You, Lord, for being the most excellent parent. May I turn to You for guidance in raising the children You have given to me. My help comes from You, the maker of Heaven and earth, and the maker of my babies. Thank You for these gifts, dear Lord. May I never try to mother them in my own strength. Help me to read the Bible and gain clear instruction. May I daily turn to You in prayer. In Jesus' name, amen.*

# Notes

1. Elisabeth Elliot, *Through Gates of Splendor* (New York: Pyramid Publications for the Christian Herald Paperback Library by arrangement with Harper & Row Publishers, Incorporated, 1956), 19.

2. René de Vries, "Corrie Ten Boom," *Heroes of the Past, Examples for the Future: Dutch Women During World War Two.* ©2002. *//hometiscali.nl/~t698467/women/corrie.htm* (December 29, 2004).

3. Amy Carmichael, *Gold Cord* (Fort Washington, PA: Christian Literature Crusade, 1932), 40.